Untidy Candles

An Anthology of Contemporary Maine Poets

Anthology: fr. Gk. anthos (flower)   logia (gathering, selecting)

Julie Zimmerman, Editor

Irene Howe, Assistant Editor

Illustrations by R.S.
This book is printed on recycled paper.

Library of Congress Catalog Card No. 94-74204
ISBN 1-879418-17-7

Published in the United States of America
        Biddle Publishing Company
        PO Box 1305
        Brunswick, Maine 04011
        207-833-5016

To my mother, Jean Fahringer Biddle, who took me riding, riding, riding with the highwayman,

And to my father, Clement Biddle, who marched me up the street with the king's horses and the king's men,

This book is dedicated.

With gratitude to William Carpenter, Tony Hoagland, Kathleen Lignell, Wesley McNair, and Betsy Sholl for their superb contributions both editorial and written; to Harriet Mosher, Lee Murch, and Trudy Chambers Price from Maine Writers and Publishers Alliance for years of encouragement and support; and to Irene Howe for pulling it all together to bring the candles to light.

Julie Biddle Zimmerman

BARBED WIRE

The old wood of that winter splintered
six inches from our faces, paint globules

floating in remover's toxic jelly, belly-up.
How troublesome the smell of wood's slow rot--

to be dispelled for sure -- and yet -
it's hard to hate it, not completely,

not the scent of cellulose relaxing,
the faint seductive whiff of letting go.

My hands cramped around the sanding block,
paint brush, putty knife. Sheet rock's white

snow drifted like a premonition in my hair.
One late March Sunday, we woke still tired

to rain ponding on the melting driveway ice,
the revelations of last year's unraked leaves.

Our voices roughened, pocked and eaten back
like corn snow slumped between the barns.

The truck gleamed in the rain.

Then Tumbledown in May's hot sun, birch buds
knotting like barbed wire. So frail a fencing —

were we in or out? Snow evened up the hollows
but the tarn was glittering, free of ice.

I declined the second summit, turned
my cheek toward speckled rock and slept.

When I woke up, you were just emerging from trees
across the saddle, as tall as they and leaning

just as they, except toward the wind, so far away
nothing distinguished you from them at all

except your movement, purposeful and quick.
I need to speak of it, how apart we were,

how much a part of the moving world.
I need to relate again the way the fields

heaped up with green, the lupines lit
untidy candles. We washed the windows,

the painters came. I want to speak of it
the way the paint flowed, white as milk.

K.M. Hooke

TABLE OF CONTENTS

INTRODUCTION

Five Maine poets who have led poetry workshops for the Maine Writers and Publishers Alliance (MWPA) were invited to contribute essays sharing their unique feelings and experiences about teaching and writing poetry in Maine. They also helped in the selection process of the poetry included by chosing from poems written by participants in one or more of their MWPA sponsored workshops or retreats.

The poetry included in this anthology represents contemporary poets living in every part of Maine as well as those who have lived here and carry a part of Maine inside them.

INTRODUCTION

AN EAR OF ONE'S OWN

It must be six or seven years ago now that Harriet Mosher called from MWPA to ask if I would do one of the Saturday workshops in poetry. About ten of us met upstairs in the old building on Mason Street and had such a good time that we planned a reunion. MWPA was kind enough to host us a second time, and we have been meeting every six or seven weeks since then. It's never exactly the same group and never entirely different. Each session includes newcomers and old hands, poets from college age to those who remember the Wright Brothers and the Spanish-American War. The workshop principles are frank and democratic. Everyone gets to speak (except the poet) and everyone's opinion is equally valued.

We've been together long enough to know one another's work, to watch each experiment, develop and mature within a critical but basically supportive framework. Poets will come for four or five straight sessions, then disappear only to return in a year or two with a fresh vision. Others come once and check it out, finding that it's not for them. What has impressed me is the spirit of seriousness and levity, tolerance and keen criticism: the welcoming of poetry, without prejudice, in all its forms and disguises.

The philosophy of our workshop is based on endless revision, weeding the poem over and over to free it from unnecessary foliage while nurturing the sprouts of choice. I find that beginning Poets often can't tell their best passages from their lesser ones. By hearing the spontaneous commentary of fellow writers, poets learn to distinguish the aspects of their own talent that can excite and dazzle an audience. Gradually over the course of a workshop, the voice of the external reader gets internalized into a critical voice in the writer's mind which becomes an inner personal accompaniment to the creative process. The workshop has to be very delicate on this issue. If the spirit of critique is too heavy, the creative side can be overwhelmed and the product gets stiff and timid as a result. We try to find and celebrate what is best in another's poem, and we discover our own vision has broadened as a result.

The poets represented here show the range of interest and experience which has characterized this diverse group. Some are published poets already; for others this is their first publication. Some are formally educated in literature and creative writing, others are self-trained or trained in other professions—lawyers, physicians, counselors, teachers, librarians. Some have Maine DNA, others are definitely from away. All are bound by their love of poetry and the attentiveness to the sound and shape of language that makes a poet.

In reading the poems submitted for this anthology, I remember many as they first appeared in the group circle, read aloud timidly or proudly by the author, courteously by a second reader, then discussed until the group had in some sense made it their own. I have come to see the workshops in another light, somewhat obstetrically, as the place where private internal events are allowed to become external, and public. Beneath the current of workshop discourse, we have felt the complex emotions of birth: the compromise between interior and external worlds, the difficulty of letting something stand on its own and go forth into the hands of others, the unsaid presence of pain, joy, and pride that accompanies anything being born.

Most of us are in Maine to fulfill some notion of community. One of the strongest of these is the community of writers. I want to thank MWPA for providing the place, continuity, and support for making such a community grow, of which this book is only one visible result.

William Carpenter

DISPLACEMENTS: SOME NOTES ON THE PURSUIT OF POETRY

All I have to do is close my eyes and I'm in church. I might be sitting in a doctor's waiting room, or riding the bus, or in a committee meeting, or at a lecture that doesn't especially interest me— some circumstance that is <u>killing</u> time. (Valery says that when we kill time we injure eternity.) All I have to do is close my eyes and hear one of the poems in my memory—by Frank O'Hara, Stanley Kunitz, Paul Goodman, Auden, or Stevens—and time is redeemed. Are these poets my friends, or my masters? I don't know. Certainly they are my rescuers. Williams says, in his great, great poem

14

"Asphodel"

> ...Today
> I'm filled with the fading memory of those flowers
>> that we both loved,
>>> even to this poor
> colorless thing-
> ...little prized among the living
>> but the dead see,
>>> asking among themselves:
> What do I remember
>> that was shaped
>>> as this thing is shaped?
> while our eyes fill
>> with tears.
>>> Of love, abiding love
>
> it will be telling...

What is it about those lines of Willliams that causes me to weep with both joy and grief? Their passion, their beauty, the truth of a human singing in a human voice about the height and depth of human life. Loss, and death, and the beauty that remains, and the strength implicit in going on. I know that I am dead,—I've perished in so many ways—and I also believe that I am living. I want to live. I pick that flower, the asphodel, and try to remember what living was like. I feel united with all others who know they are not living, but who remember life. Williams' poem is about many things, but one of its subjects is poetry itself, what it can do, its value in human experience.

What Williams does for me, and what so much beloved poetry does, is exactly what religion has done for human experience for countless ages—it places its fingers on the keys, and sounds the notes of the human condition: memory opens its doors and rushes in, hope opens its still-young throat and sings; love and grief circle like spirits in the air. Feeling flows back into the numb extremities.

15

The dead are risen, and honored, and the wreath is laid in the right place. One of Frank O'Hara's poems is titled "In Memory of My Feelings." Poetry is the memory of my feelings.

Yesterday morning I read with two other writers in the Colby College student union as part of a benefit for the Maine Food Bank. What a funny idea, to barter literature for food! The writer before me, novelist Rick Russo, read a wonderfully written, hilarious passage about a boy coercing his parents into buying him a dog. It was such a pleasure to listen to him work his changes on language that I forgot my own anxiety about performing.

It is a thing I've noticed before, but it still amazes: how any work of art must, and can, during the period of its performance, displace every other work of art that has ever been created. While a good story or poem is being read, or listened to, Shakespeare doesn't exist. Dickens doesn't exist. Michelangelo doesn't exist. The work at hand, in the air, on the page, or on the canvas, is the dominant dream that holds us in the rapture of attention. The whole volume and history of great art is annihilated, if the art of the moment is sufficient, is good. This is the great democracy of art, when the spell is well-cast. It is not that Russo is better than Dickens or Shakespeare; it is that his craft and vision earn their moment, win their place, which, like the moment, is both temporary and eternal. In one of Rilke's early poems, addressed to God, he says, "You are the moment at twilight that makes all poets equal."

What is that quality in a poetic voice, in a poem, that makes that Herculean, magical act of displacement, that shouldering aside of all previous art, possible? It isn't Suffering, and it isn't Wisdom; we all have suffered and many Wise Ones are not good writers. Lately the term <u>Freshness</u> has been resonant for me: directness, immediacy. I want a poem to address me in a voice that is freshly, complexly human. I want to know that somebody is home, inhabiting that poem. Ironically, though, I can't help but recognize that such habitation depends on a great deal of Art—artifice, technique: rhetoric, diction, syntax, wordplay. That is what I tell my students these days. An incalculable amount of art goes into the artlessness of "Asphodel," or the beginning of Berryman's Dreamsong #4:

> Life, friends, is boring. We must not say so.
> After all, the sky flashes, the great sea yearns,
>
> we ourselves flash and yearn...

Berryman was, among many other things, a Shakespeare scholar. But that doesn't mean erudition is necessary to write great poems. Guts are probably as important as Artfulness. My friend Marie says that poetry is simply saying out loud the thing you most don't want to say. Real, inhabited, Fresh poems are being written successfully all the time. It is happening even now, among us. It is the great paradox of writing that in order to have the nerve to actually put ink on our own paper, we have to forget everything that has been done before, how often and how well. At the same time, we ideally are informed by the whole history of our reading, the whole history of poetry, as well as the history of our experience. This paradox accounts for the enormous, indissoluble, acrobatic, athletic feat of a real poem, one that has both Art and Immediacy.   At the recent

17

Maine Writers Fall Retreat, I was moved by my students in many ways: by their humble willingness to study a great art form with admiration rather than covetousness. By their lack of competitiveness. By their visible sense of gratitude simply to be, for that weekend, writers talking and thinking about writing. The freedom they felt from the rest of their "real-world" identities as husbands, wives, parents, psychologists, teachers was visibly a deep pleasure for them. Studenthood demands humility; practice requires stubbornness and egotism, includes loneliness and repeated failure. Why does one want to make a poem? Not merely out of egotism, but as a way to prove that we lived. To tell other people (and ourselves, of course) who we are, what it was like. To prove that it was not a lonely and forgettable dream.

>   Of love, abiding love
>   it will be telling...
>
>   There is something
>   something urgent
>   I have to say to you
>   and you alone
>   but it must wait
>   while I drink in
>   the joy of your approach...

All I have to do is close my eyes and I'm in church. If you look behind the pulpit, where the Pretenders like to stand, you'll find a door. If you open the door, you'll find a room where a lot of real people live—no more real than us. Stevens is playing his Moog synthesizer. Frank O'Hara is yakking on the telephone. Rilke is staring bleakly out the window. There is a pool where you can see

the outline of Keats' lip-prints in the water— fresh as the day he
pressed them there.

Tony Hoagland

LETTER TO EMILY D.

Dear Emily,

This is a letter of complaint. I've had it with your New
England winters and your "certain slant of light." It's all over with us,
even though we have so much in common. Our birthdays nearly
coincide this week, although I'm only about a fourth your age. But
I'm old enough to begin to see winter the way you did in your poems.
I see what you were talking about when you wrote about winter
afternoons with their oppressive slant of light.

Maybe I'll never be able to "see New Englandly," because
here I am this winter afternoon, in my long johns and five layers of
wool and thinsulate, standing in two feet of snow with the wind
whipping around my head and a chill factor of minus-30 degrees,
and trying to be philosophical about all this.

Besides which, you must remember I grew up in the San
Francisco Bay Area: a place of dazzling-bright winter light, stark
white skyscrapers, sailboats on the Bay in December, and startling
sunsets. A frontier mentality with a penchant for directness and
clarity and "saying it like it is." I imagine this is why I prefer un-

adorned and unornamented poetry, both in myself and others.

I suppose there is something in my Scottish/German blood which distrusts the Baroque, the gorgeous, the Mediterranean gush of feeling, thinking there is something vaguely dishonest in using art and poetry for an outburst of unbridled passion. Give me Williams or Rilke any time; I just don't seem to have the urge for Italy or Greece that ignited the Romantics like Keats and Byron and Shelley.

So maybe we have more in common than I thought. Maybe there's something of the New Englander in me, after all. I, too, yearn for the plain style, finding the uncommon in the common, the extraordinary in the ordinary, confirmation in the unconfirmed, presence in what first seems like absence.

I've nearly finished shoveling out my car, and your lines are going over and over in my head about that certain slant of light "Winter afternoons....When it comes, the Landscape listens---/ Shadows----hold their breath."

I find myself stopping to watch my ice-cold breath and contemplating the stillness in the midst of the fierce wind. And I find myself, like you did, thinking about this frigid landscape of light invading my body like an icy shadow.

I am so cold it's hard to make myself scrape off the ice on the windshield, but I know that as long as you move, you are alive. So I force myself to keep moving. I stomp my feet and do a burly dance of the icewoman and I know I must look ridiculous to the drivers passing by.

I envy the birds flying low over the mudflats, how they are made for flight. When the going gets rough, they flap their wings

20

and head off in the direction of a different season, where there's more sunlight, longer days, and shorter nights. Should I imitate them, I wonder, as I imagine myself lying on a sunny beach somewhere south of the border.

But that southern world with its harsh sunlight suddenly seems forced, unreal, glitzy. I think again of your certain slant of light. It's the oppressiveness or some nagging fear of despair that you were hinting at, some finality, some hint of death. Some undeniable truth of the season. By going south, seeking escape, snowbirding it for the sun belt, we deny the seasons of ourselves.

Again I am forced back to your poem, and I ask myself if I have learned anything from the winters of my life—from the short, nine hours of December daylight we know in northern New England. I think of how deeply my body has gasped for air in the sub-zero temperatures, how much I have craved the inner heat from the woodstove, how the house and land provide sustenance even on the days the power goes out and the telephone lines go down in an ice storm. Those days are hard and etched in memory. They require all the labor of my experience, both bone-chilling and frightening. They have taught me more about the landscape and the resilience of my body to work for its survival than anything else I've known.

And I realize that the meaning of my life has come from these hard places, where I have had to labor most, in that certain slant of light on winter afternoons out in the wind and blowing snow, working to free my car. It's out here in the oppressive cold light where I am most human, using both body strength and mind to fend off the numbing cold, going past coldness into the larger thoughts, where death becomes possibility and where life becomes more valuable than it was twenty minutes earlier inside my house.

It's a choice I can make, after all: either to return inside to the security of the house or to stay outside in the world and bring the metaphor of winter light into fulfillment, into reality. Knowing that to move is to be alive, to change oneself, to transform. By recognizing the slant of light, the indirectness of its glow, I recognize how things deepen into revelation.

In direct light, everything is exposed. Direct light gives no opportunity for mystery, for shadow, for change. But the winter's "certain slant of light" is a frontier landscape, one that must be challenged.

So maybe I owe you an apology, Emily. Maybe you'll never allow me to escape New England. Maybe I've just been looking for the words to thank you for showing me how "to see New Englandly"—which is to say, *indirectly*. Which is to say, *wild, slanted, northern*.

Cordially,
Kathleen

P.S. I hope the weather where you are is clement now.
Is it true that you considered Walt Whitman a "flimflam" artist?

Kathleen Lignell

THINKING THE SENTENCE

Imagine Walt Whitman or Emily Dickinson with pencils sharpened waiting in a class of their peers to be shown how to do creative writing, and you'll see how silly it is to assume that workshops can make poets. All we teachers of poetry writing can really manage is to show the techniques poets use in their art and to shore up the confidence of those who study with us. The rest is up to our students' inspirations.

What did I say about poetic techniques in my MWPA workshop on free verse? Quite honestly, I don't remember, but I may have mentioned, as I often do, the origins of linebreaks in ordinary conversation. Whenever we speak about something that matters to us, something that involves us in earnest thought, I tell my students, we speak in line-breaks, and I illustrate the idea by the pauses in my own sentence as I utter it. If we don't hear linebreaks when another person talks to us, I add, or if the linebreaks are programmatic, we know we're listening to a political speech or a commercial.

My point is that my students have arrived with skills basic to the workshop already in hand. They have not only spoken their own sentences line by line, but they are aware of the linebreak as a stress one gives to the sentence as one thinks it—aware, too, of how a sentence in motion can help us make up our minds. The object of the workshop, then, is to refine the skills they have brought with them.

One way I might help them do this is to pass out free verse by well-known poets, having printed the free verse as prose. My students' task, with a few clues about the number of stanzas and lines in the authors' poems, is to shape the prose into poetry, alert to the interplay of the line and the sentence, the music of that interplay, and the way a poem may touch against the space around itself as it moves on the page, making that wordlessness articulate also. From time to time, I might give examples of effective syntax in poetry, citing sentences by poets like Keats, Dickinson, Frost, Williams, Bishop, and Rich that unfold in a conditional and somewhat wild way, showing how predictable and dull the sentences of contemporary verse—which tend to start with the verb rather than delaying it—often are. What I am hoping in all of this talk of how to make a poem whose lines reveal the pressure of thought thinking itself, and whose sentences unfold with an oblique rightness, is that my students will one day happen on subjects that engage them so profoundly, they'll be forced to use all the skills I have given them and even more. What I'm hoping is that they'll be carried by their inspiration in the way Frost describes in his famous essay "The Figure a Poem Makes":

> For me the initial delight is in the surprise of
> remembering something I didn't know I knew.
> I am in a place, in a situation, as if I had mater-
> ialized from cloud or risen out of the ground.
> There is a glad recognition of the long lost
> and the rest follows. Step by step the un-
> expected supply keeps growing....
> It must be more felt than seen ahead like
> prophesy. It must be a revelation, or a
> series of revelations, as much for the poet

as for the reader. For it to be that there
must have been the greatest freedom of
the material to move about in it and to
establish relations in it regardless of time
and space, previous relation, and everything
but affinity.

After all, how could I hope for my students anything less
than I hope for myself?

Wesley McNair

TRUSTING THE UNCONSCIOUS

Since writing is a solitary activity using the basic material of
social discourse, it seems inevitable that certain tensions are built
in—between solitude and community, between the elation of starting
new work and the more studied critical act of revision, between our
conflicting impulses toward being generous and territorial. Don't we
long for time alone to write—that sweet mania of being the mad
scientist in our own private labs? But then, what we create in
language has social implications. Someone has to get the irony.
Heartbreak has to break hearts.

Probably the most helpful workshops encourage individual-
ity, giving poets permission to discover their own particular obses-
sions and weirdnesses, their heartbreak passions. Czeslaw Milosz
says we are "always pupils in an introductory class," and I think
successful workshops make us feel the wisdom and joy of that. We

accept the way art requires of us perpetual student status, a life-long apprenticeship to the tradition, the language and the world around us.

While I certainly value workshops in which the goal is to fine-tool poems brought from home and to discuss principles of craft, I've always felt a little cheeky critiquing the work of people I don't know. So at the MWPA fall retreats I structured the workshops around the idea of generating new material. I'd bring in a range of exercises, some playful, others more serious, and we'd spend the weekend writing and discussing the results with each other. It wasn't a matter of getting things right, but of exploring, learning from each other the way imagination and language work. There was such an energy bath in the room, I'd look up expecting to see bodies glowing, in spite of the almost inevitable rain falling in the woods outside.

If I had to justify this more generative approach, I'd say its main value is as an object lesson on trusting the unconscious elements of art and the powers of language itself. The clarity and shape that poems require have deep roots in the unconscious mind where strange and wonderful associations occur. We need to know that and trust it, so that when we are alone working we'll have the patience to wait on the poem. Revision involves skepticism, but first we have to compose. Another value of such workshops is that they move us a little closer to the experience of jamming. We weren't exactly bebop musicians there in the woods, but the process of composition became a little more improvisational, loose—something

26

useful to have recorded in the brain stem, for when we write our-
selves into a tight spot back home. We also created a kind of
community in those sessions where we felt ourselves to be more
advocates than competitors. Our ambitions were for the poems, not
ourselves. It reminds me of the way several visual artists will share
space—one of those big rooms with drop cloths and dusty window
light, people at different stages of production, the whole place in
flux, process, work happening.

Of course, there's a long middle period in the composition of
a poem, where the poet needs to remain alone, listening hard to his
or her inner voices. The poem at this stage is pre-social or even
anti-social, and doesn't need anybody else's advice. Closer to the
end of the process, when it's time to step back and have a more
detached perspective, the hard questions begin. Or maybe they've
always been there, troubling the waters of our minds, and now we
have to consciously act on them. I don't really worry what the rest of
the world thinks of poetry. I worry about myself, and whether I'm
facing the dangers of copping out. Have I gone slack? Am I rewrit-
ing the same old poem I already know how to make? Is there a turn
I missed, a challenge I'm avoiding? That's what I need other writers
for—the risks they take, their flexibility and humor when I have
none, the thing in their work we call "vision" or "depth," when lan-
guage starts to transform, leap toward wisdom.

As to the tension between generosity and our more territorial
instincts—it certainly exists. Sometimes in workshops I am re-
minded of my first Lamaze class, where I was shocked to see a

27

room full of pregnant women, after being the only one I'd known for eight months. What deflation. And what relief. Sometimes people at different stages of development can appall each other with their bluntness or extreme sensitivity. And hard questions are harder if somebody else asks them when the poet's not ready. I remind myself that any attitude surfacing in the workshop's microcosm, probably exists in the larger literary world. I've also found that it's often my toughest critics who have been most helpful in getting me to see poems in a new way— even if I discover this alone in some corner licking my wounds.

But, back to the pleasures of the workshop, the writer's working society. There's the sudden clarifying perspective on a poem we've long struggled over, the new insight about craft, or renewed courage to push ourselves a little harder. There's the relief of being with others also trying to balance this thing called a writer's life. There's the pleasure of improvising, writing things we wouldn't have written without that exercise or this group, the kind of wild card experimentation that thrives on random associations. Because so much of what we do is lonelier than this, MWPA workshops offer a rare and precious sense of community. I can close my eyes and still see the room. Rain falling outside. Inside people sitting on couches and lawn chairs, reading what they have just written. It seems almost miraculous that so much different energy and coherence and beauty could well up in one room. Like pregnant women lined up on the floor trying to pant and relax at once, we're together for a while, knowing that soon enough we'll each be alone again with our labors

of love.

Betsy Sholl

Biographical Notes

William Carpenter has published three books of poetry including *Rain* and *Speaking Fire at Stones* as well as a novel, *A Keeper of Sheep*. In 1972 he helped found the College of the Atlantic where he now teaches. His numerous awards include the AWP's Contemporary Poetry Award, the Samuel French Morse Prize, and a National Endowment for the Arts grant.

Tony Hoagland, who currently teaches at Colby College, has published three chapbooks and contributed to three anthologies as well, *New American Poets of the 90's, Best of Crazyhorse*, and *The Pushcart Anthology, 1991*. He has just been recognized with the John C. Zacharis First Book Award for *Sweet Ruin*.

Kathleen Lignell, a poet, writer, editor, and translator, teaches literature and creative writing at the University of Maine at Orono. She has traveled extensively in Mexico and received the Pablo Neruda Poetry Award from *Nimrod* and a NEA fellowship. Her published works include *The Calamity Jane Poems* and a novel, *The White Buffalo*. She was an editor of *The Eloquent Edge: 15 Maine Women Writers*.

Wesley McNair received grants from the Rockefeller, Fulbright and Guggenheim Foundations and NEH and NEA Fellowships for Creative Writers. He has won the Devins Award for poetry, the Eunice Tietjens Prize from *Poetry* and Theodore Roethke Prize from *Poetry Northwest*. His script for the PBS series on Robert Frost took a New England Emmy Award. The most recent of his four published books of poetry is *My Brother Running*.

Betsy Sholl has been living in Portland for 11 years. Besides MWPA workshops, she teaches at the University of Southern Maine and in the Vermont College MFA Program. She was the 1991 winner of the Maine Chapbook competition with *Pick a Card*. *The Red Line*, which won the 1991 AWP award for poetry, is the most recent of her four published volumes.

POEMS

Ruth Bookey

NIGHTMARES

In Maine
Dad is still pursued
by uniforms.

Mother tries
to mend old slacks
brought from Germany.
Worn seams keep opening up.

Running for her flight
my middle-aged sister's bag falls open
—junior high school clothes spill.

In a dark city—shrouded,
a small woman limps toward me.
But my mother is tall.

THE POWER OF IT

Ruth woke sad today. Life, she says,
has been behaving itself and hopeful
expectations continue. So why now a
nameless dread and mope at sunrise?
What is it?

To help her against
it—whatever it is
I hold her in my arms,
and I tell her what it is is
that there come moments
when it is simply it.

I say this as much
for myself as for her
—that it is just it.

And it helps.

Emily Rand Breitner

TRANSFORMATIONS

Snapshot:
The old apple tree lifts
its drift
of snow above tentative green
in the upswing
season.

In today's dim light
you may think that
the white wood chips
around the stump
were petals,
but there's no mistaking
the trail the beavers made dragging
apple branches downslope: Route 1
skids into a water lane
outlined in ice.

Across
the glass pond a lodge juts
from the shore. Drifts of white sift

onto its igloo roof, beavers and kits watertight.

Their freezer's full and snow,

falling snow.

A benediction.

Nancy Brown Stump

THE COWRIE

The shrunken man is strapped into bed and allowed no weapons
like a comb or brush to allay his demons; even the light cord
is gone since he wrapped it three times tight around his neck.

His daughter's daughter brings a shiny shell he nods to.
She puts it in his hand and he pops it in his mouth like
chocolate. Whispers leak out its pale toothed lips.

He tastes salt water breathing and swallows the prayers and
curses of drowning men. Long ago, he might have died at sea,
but he was saved for this.

After the child has left, he will join the others, pressing
this gift, his daughter's blessing, down his throat to stop
his breath. Starvation takes too long.

Paul Butler

THE ARROGANCE OF STONE

Below the surface of the dark lake,
the white face of a whiskered catfish
eating Dad's ashes
as I poured them into the water,
the orange of the sunset
coming in a line to me
across black waves.
I recall saying to him
out here on the lake
when I was sixteen:
"I'm afraid I don't want to be anything, Dad,"
to which he said, "Any thing — that's good!"
Mother buried some of his ashes
under a polished granite gravestone
where I've been only once, at dusk.
The moon came up through leafless November trees.
I saw myself deep in the stone, its words across my face.

Joan Detel

WINTER IN THE WOODS

The winter wood's
a lot like love,
all those branches, trunks
and twigs, so stark, so bare,
yet still so dense and close.
It's hard to tell
what will last and leaf,
and what will snap and break
in December cold
to be picked up
for kindling
next year.

Nancy Devine

SHE COULDN'T HELP HERSELF

I've been thinking about
my dead mother
these summer days, as I watch
the daisies come and go.
The tight swirled pattern
of their yellow nipples
strikes me as another
double helix, those swirls
we bear in our own
seed, so striking and compact.
Over time, the daisies
push out until the pattern
is gone, leaving
a nappy breast
at the center of each one,
fuzzy as the overused
upholstery of that easychair
my mother sat in, nursing
her bruised feelings and her after-dinner
scotch while my father watched
television in the other room, and she
listened to all of those hopelessly
romantic tunes she couldn't
help herself from loving.

Robert W. Edson

WHALE WATCH

Fifteen miles across and nine hundred feet deep,
the Saint Lawrence swelled to shore,
frothing together at the Sanguenay Fiord,
its truncated tide losing ground inch by inch
as the sea became a river.

In the great feeding ground of Tadoussac,
flashes of white Beluga whales mixed with white caps
so I had to strain my eyes
to tell who was paired or alone.

At six in the morning of the last day,
I watched the full moon sink into the mountains,
slipping away slice by slice,
becoming a snowcap, then melting into memory.

Behind me, Riviere-du-Loup still slept,
its skyline pierced by church spires
competing with television towers for dominance,
the past arguing with the future.

I bent to the cool earth
and picked a daisy out of habit,
then got on the idling bus
waiting to take me back to Maine.

Lisa Giles

THE OUTER BANKS — CAPE HATTERAS II

I walk the grasspath alone.
Someone sings at my ear
but I don't turn to see who it is.

There is a moon
striking the clearing
that is wide enough
only for my body.

I walk headdown,
shoulders lowered,
braced into a stride
that covers more ground
more quickly.

Sunset seems hours ago
and now the crickets
rub their legs incessantly,
the pitch so high
it dissolves into air,
almost.

Perhaps it is the crickets
at my ear, tempting me,
perhaps it is you.

Jim Ham

NIGHT LIGHT

Up in the sky
a glow
a light in the night
like the second coming—
of something,
I didn't know
could have been
Jesus Christ Rubinowitz,
Mohammed himself
or just a silo gone hay-wire
out in Nevada.
It was something at least
that I wasn't quite sure of.
Could have been meteorite
full of positive energy
that took a wrong-turn
to here
attracted magnetically
toward us
through Earth's negativity.
That's what I thought
but found out later
it wasn't that heavenly—
the dump was on fire.

Anne Hammond

TUPELO CREEK BOTTOM

Crouching
I can see
Just understory
Impenetrable vines and stems
In humid heat.

Somewhere
If I get low enough
I might find
The creek that flows here
Source of all this exuberance.

The eye would love to travel its length
The feet to follow
Its muddy allure
Where a maple flower may lie
Or a coon's step be recorded.

But wise ones have been here before me.
The chain link fence stands eight feet tall
Between the houses and the trickling rill.
No exit.
No entrance.

And someone is building a pile of trash

Paper plates, bottles

A child's bicycle and

Plastic things flow over the bank.

The elite believe this useless rivulet

Must be fenced and

Trashed

Hidden completely

Following nature's example.

Not knowing this

The thrush seeks its nesting place

Here in the threading vines

Behind the sanitary-air hotel

And the southern homes.

Arresting birdsong

Floats above it all

Refusing to cease.

Crouch down.

Judith Harris

THE MARSH

Who can comprehend the dignity
of an autumn marsh gathering sunlight?
The birds unknowing ornament her reeds.
To claim such calm as this on a clear day
is something I can scarce imagine.
My greedy flesh, the craven want
that flaunts my flaws, calls me
down with a falconer's control
and I am bled of innocence.
Yet, even so, beside this marsh
there sings in me some
sweet, wild sensibililty
that remembers the sky
and longs to fly like a golden bird
up from the silent reeds.

DRIVING AT NIGHT

Driving at night, don't the lighted
windows still draw you in? Slouched
in the back seat, once you imagined
the lives inside lit up so much

brighter than your own. Now it's you
behind the wheel of this vehicle
hurtling through darkness. It's you
still hoping for a view, a slice

of someone else's life. So what
if it's no more than a glimpse
of Mrs. Robinson in the bath
examining a patch of skin?

It may not be silk, but you feel
sure she lives in it more comfortably
that you do in yours. Just as you're
sure that if you could lift one wall

of each house on this street to see
why your neighbors draw their blinds,

you'd find Mr. Allen wearing
something from Victoria's Secret

and your lawyer getting funky
with some loud music in his mirror.
And you at home still thinking how
easy it would have been, at your

cousin's wedding, to slip into that
drunken conga line. Well, you slide
the top back on your lipstick. Step away
from the mirror, smile as you descend

and no-one but the cats to take
you in. You are your own watchful neighbor,
living always beside yourself.
It gets tiring. Here's another

sun down, another melancholy
twilight. But doesn't the road
gleam a little, doesn't it rise
above the darkening ground?

Your car moves along it as lights
come on in living rooms and kitchens
all the way into town. And you, inside,
are finally invisible.

K.M. Hooke

LUNCH WITH MY SISTER

We want her to cut her hair —
that torn dark mist that drifts
unsurely toward her shoulders —

we want her to wear socks
in winter and shoes instead
of these blue sneakers, K-Mart, $9.99,

whose graying warp already shows
one toe worrying through the canvas.
For years we wanted her to take a bath,

to throw out the multi-colored cardigan
whose buttons hung like grimy medals
and whose elbows had been worn

to crimps of brown and yellow yarn
that lost from year to year
their tight-knit memories.

But that was before this polite young man,
twelve years her junior, who sits with us
in the renovated-yet-again In Town Cafe,

a fourth cup of coffee shaking
in his hands, asking if it's all right
if he has another Pepsi, while she watches him,

keeps his cigarettes, feeds him onion rings.
Ersatz country paper covers the cafe walls
like blemish cream; a few straw wreaths

warm the vault-like space the way
a candle would a barn. Oldies radio,
Connie Francis, "Stupid Cupid".

That cold north bedroom, ice edging up
the inside glass. "Do you remember," I ask,
"the singing contests we used to have,

we'd imitate Connie Francis, Brenda Lee,
then rate each other, who was best?"
A forest of mascara hedges her blue eyes.

The old floor boards are trembling.
For a moment, I see them as if from below,
stretched hollow as a canvas, the center

coming apart, beams tumbling in space,
end over end, above our upturned faces,
coming down. He grins, apologetic.

"It's just me, jiggling my feet."
We want her to be wary and not to spend
her meager money on his cigarettes

and Pepsis, we want her to be circumspect,
sexually responsible, and maybe
she could take her coat off indoors,

and if not cut her hair, at least
tie it back and not wear so much
streaked make-up that the waitress

coming with the check looks at her
and him and hands the check to me
with a look of what's supposed to be

understanding that excludes the two of them.
Most of all, we want her to be seventeen
again and beautiful, second in her class,

student council president, cheerleader
in the thick wool sweater
that I stole from time to time.

We want her to go through the university
in four years this time instead of five,
without the rages and hallucinations,

the shock treatments and committals.
And I want back my anger at perfection,
I want to hear her voice again,

hanging like an icicle in the dark
across from me, first her thin voice,
then mine. He smiles at her.
There is milkshake on his chin.
She holds a napkin out, dark hair swaying
like a climber's ropes.

Irene Howe

IN EACH VESSEL

I don't know how often she does this,
but she's outside again mumbling to herself
as she does when she thinks no one can hear.

Her gray head's bowed hoping, through sheer
force of will to undo the weight of snow upon
snow constricting into itself so she can set
the flowers free.

She has the eyes of Michelangelo as he tries
to penetrate marble, discover the form waiting
within, and chisel the vision true.

Somewhere deep inside she remembers
the lost tribe who long ago knew enough
to create each piece of pottery with an extra
opening so the spirit within each vessel would
not be trapped.

So she's out there again in the cold, talking
herself through her days in some primitive
tongue, probing the depths of each day's details
searching for the opening.

Meredith Hutchins

INHERITANCE

This chest of drawers I'm painting
Must be nearly fifty years old.
Father built it from scraps of wood
And painted it green, his favorite color.
For years it stood beside the kitchen door,
Top drawer stuffed with mittens. Then,
Re-painted brown, it was moved to a
Bedroom to hold underwear and socks.
Age has assigned it a seasonal
Patronage, here in the summer cottage,
Where annually I do a bout of
Unskilled maintenance and repair.

I have no bent for building and painting,
Unlike the rest of my family.
They shingled roofs, varnished trim,
Fixed cars, built boats. A practical
People, none of them wrote poetry.
Except....there was some distant cousin,
Too peripheral to have a name,
Who'd sometimes join the men
Around the stove in grandfather's shop.
They always spoke of him with a laugh,

And could only recall the preface
That attended his recitations,
How every time he'd begin by saying
He'd found this poem in the road.

Sharon Junken

SONNET FOR A WEAVER

I see you glorious, grieving in the room
amid the warp, the weft, the branching frame.
Outpouring love a tangle in the loom.
Each shuttle cross, a lovecross borne in pain.

Your hands so white and strong against the black
of destiny's directive, premature.
With darkest blue you summon spirit back,
attempt with yarn, bind soul to body sure.

What trial sore to weave that last request!
Sad tears and skeins entwined within your heart.
The task demanded soul's most wrenching test;
to unify as you were pulled apart.

Beloved friend, ennobled brave in duty,
from chilling thoughts, created warming beauty.

CAST IRON BATHTUB DREAM

I lie in a high cast iron bathtub.
My hands rest on the curved lip.
The hot, soapy water is up to my nipples.

In the floor length mirror, which is mounted
On the bathroom door,
I see the eagle claw feet of the tub.

The tub's feet begin to move.
The bathroom door opens, and the tub
Walks out of the bathroom, with me in it.

The bathtub runs down the stairs quickly.
The heavy front door swings open,
And we (the tub and I) are outside, in the sunlight.

The bathtub is running through the woods,
But the water in the tub remains calm.
The wind in my face is exhilarating.

Faster and faster we run, down a winding path
Through the woods, past giant hemlocks,
Blueberry bushes, and orange lilies.

Presently, we are running across a meadow
Of daisies, black-eyed Susans, and Queen Anne's Lace.
In the background, there is piano music.

It is one of Bartok's fast Hungarian
Peasant Songs, played loudly.
The flowers bend and sway to the wild music.

The path through the dancing meadow
Approaches the top of a cliff. As the tub
Runs heedlessly toward the cliff, I am worried.

The bathtub picks up speed, and at the edge
Of the cliff, it leaps into space,
And we fly, we soar, we glide.

Far below us, I see the top of the forest,
A thick green rug, and I see
Long blue snakes, twisting across the land.

I pull the rubber plug, and drape the plug chain
Over the faucets. Cold, clear drops of rain
Fall from the drain. I hear songbirds' bubbling calls.

We fly lower. A crowd of people has gathered
In a field. They are looking up at us.
They stretch out their arms, as the rain falls on them.

The faucets are turned on. Hot water runs
Into the tub. Cold, clear rain water runs

Out of the drain. I do not question this.

We approach the village. In my

Cast iron, airborne chariot, I glide

Triumphantly over the rooftops.

There are hundreds of church steeples.

We weave through a forest of spires.

Night falls, and starlight sparkles on tin steeple roofs.

Myrna Koonce

FOG AT POPHAM BEACH

Expecting sun, we find instead this quiet blindness,

a cloud to lay the blanket in

and wander through without a compass.

Whatever lies closest becomes all there is:

the clamshell's palm-fitting curve, or sand

soft as cornstarch, lining a tidal pool.

Somewhere, a dog barks,

reverberations stilled by air pregnant with water,

pregnant without hope of birth.

Is this what waiting felt like,

before the final heave into pure air,

unbearable light? A suspension,

sounds muffled, an edgeless world

until some downward pressure bore us out?

Compelled by rhythm, we walk

toward and toward the breaking waves,

the narrow arc of sand before us

unchanging; we seem to come no nearer.

As if from nowhere the dog bounds up,

black as we knew he would be,

a solid wraith. And gone

again, unrestrained, black swallowed

by white. We reach

the waves spreading their scalloped foam,

stoop to run our fingers through liquid mud

that hypnotizes as it drips,

lulling us while the sun thins the mist,

revealing what we might have seen:

dune grass still tethered to its fragile roots,

least terns laying their eggs in shallow sand,

an empty lifeguard chair, its white

white arms thrusting out to sea.

Elizabeth Koopman

BREAD

My father taught me
to boil eggs:
turn on the burner, run hot water over them,
pour it off, look for cracks,
run hot water over them again,
set the timer for seven minutes.
When they boil, turn off the heat at once.
So when people ask if I like a three- or four-minute egg
I have no idea.
I think of him
up before the rest of us, making breakfast
almost until he died.
I still eat my eggs the way he used to coax me —
"little egg, little orange juice" —
to which, when we were very small,
he sometimes added sugar water, carefully made.

My mother taught me
her own salad dressing:
olive oil, safflower oil, red wine vinegar,
measured in a peanut butter jar;
dash salt, tarragon, a touch of mustard,
chop garlic, cover the surface with pepper and shake.
I see my young mother

making up recipes with her Italian roommate
in a city of adventure;
their spaghetti sauce
which I used to eat on bread —
ground lamb and Campbell's tomato soup
for lack of Italian tomato paste.

I made up my own
recipe for bread:
exact amounts of yeast, salt, and water,
a dollop of oil and honey,
and as much flower as it takes.
Knead five minutes or so.
I used to let it rise in a water bath,
temperature measured with anxious precision,
but now I just leave it on the counter.
If it's cold it takes all day,
If it's hot it's done in an hour.

My parents
never ate bread,
my mother allergic to wheat, my father
out of the habit. But he remembered
French bread, long sticks
bought in the sleepy dawn, baked overnight

in stone caverns, in the Paris of his childhood.
I never make French bread.

I still hear my mother, grown cautious,
telling me it's too hard to bake bread at all;
I still hear my father
dreaming of those grey stone mornings and the early warm scent
that offered to fill his hungry soul.

Sometimes I think it is too hard to bake bread at all.
But I have learned that my bread is easy-going
if not always an adventure.
I did bake French bread once
but I did not believe in it.

<u>Emily Lattimore</u>

PROXIMATE ANTIPHONIES

I

Dark clouds, languid, gauzy,
veiled blue-black rounded
mountains to the east

Beyond old, fragile elms
at the pond's western outlet
the sky was whiter
than silver, silver in the water

Highly indignant redwinged
blackbirds flew hard at me
from dry cattail lookouts

Frogs rang small gongs; a few,
hearing my cautious footfalls,
loud as cavalry,
plucked the sheer surface downward

Still as can be, I marked
the progress of
their roundelay

— in the fond belief
    discovery of pattern
    may assure true
    memory —

        II

Days later, under bright sun
at a smaller pond, I push
my friend's chair close
to greening cattail rushes

We hear two frogs
"If I were eight years old
I'd catch one for you..."
    —curving my hands
    to the peaked back,
    taut thighs, purse
    of breath, heart, gut

For both of us, our frog-catching
days are long over
I try to tell him
of the frogs singing in turn
round and round their silvered pond
that sultry morning
    (but never mention:
    plucked water,
    the uncaged heart's cool flutter)

Dawn Lilly

KUWAIT

Get up, switch on the war.
Americans are hot on the spot
with live, immediate coverage of US
bombing Baghdad. Hussein hunkers down
in his plush underground shelter,
rolling around on ball-bearing chairs,
safe, as he plays bait and wait.

I remember air raid alerts, World War II,
hiding behind the black Atlantic oil stove
while radio broadcasts blatted war news.

From safety, I watched gurgling oil
bubble in the inverted green-glazed bottle
as fluid released into copper tubing
fueled our main source of heat. Grandfather,
armed with black-band and billy-club,
pulled black-out shades (which were green) and
walked the streets patrolling for night raids.

Mobile scuds scoop air space over Saudi.
Patriot missiles intercept some,
others penetrate Riyadh.
War noise is deafening. Blinding flashes

explode with frightening frequency, and
I wonder why I love fireworks' displays.
I don't like this one and switch off.

The night my grandfather fell through a shaft
at U.S. Gypsum and lost his leg,
I did an acrobatic dance for the
American Legion Smith Toby Post 21.
Grandfather never saw me perform on-stage.
For years, he sat tapping his fingers on the maple-
armed chair (sometimes to music, sometimes not),
listening to Red Sox games, and smoking cigars.

Long days, he sat by that north window
patiently teaching my brother and me
to play cribbage, until we became a bit
of a challenge or thought we were.
We were the best at 15-2, 15-4
combinations in school.

The Atlantic had a large oven
to where I raced each morning,
warmed feet icy from the floors above,
reluctantly withdrew from the heat
into the kitchen chill
to wash at the black-slate sink
and quickly switch pajama-top
for Buster Brown jersey and handknit sweater
over the white, cotton undershirt

with bow
which was changed once
between weekly baths
in the round galvanized tub.

Grandfather died of throat cancer
the month I turned ten.
We moved from the oil tanks,
the wash of the Doubling Point
Light on the Kennebec, uptown
to the other side of the tracks,
an oil-fired furnace,
and a bathroom
with a porcelain lined,
cast-iron tub.

We don't have night alerts
in this accelerated age.
The BIW still builds ships here
next to the Naval Air Base.

Deborah Luhrs

THE WOMAN WHO SLEPT BESIDE A BEAR

He read a story to her
as they leaned against the couch ends,
facing the middle, at each other;
woolly-socked feet probing into the strangely
vast distance across a mere cushion.
She massaged his feet that jutted up like
small grey owls by her outer thighs,
and lizard-legged her own along his jeans,
inner thigh to the squeeze under the buttocks -
finding the tight, warm space that a
snail must feel when retreating
deeply into the shell.

The story was of a woman who married a bear -
wafting down from Alaska in a book of essays,
from Maria Johns, a native story-teller
who expressed more colorful detail in her
blindness than most people ever truly see.

Amused, she thinks of all the bear literature
that keeps finding her recently, and how
unexpectedly drawn she is to this unlikely beast.
And, why not -

She imagines them curing up into each other
for the sleep of winter, the dreaming of
abundant berries dripping from smacking lips
or the silver splash of salmon turning
into a pink afternoon feast.

Now she lay there -
between sheets of moonlight drifting
across what began as her bed, her quietly
quilted mattress on the floor under the
lowly-hung eastward window.

He lay there also -
drifting quickly into that fast sleep of men,
his bulk becoming bear-like to her
in light more crepuscular than this
moonlight striking through midnight -
as if they might be huddled in
a dimly-lit cave.

His persistent snoring becomes the
groan and growl of Ursus Arctos, ancient
creature whom man thinks he must fear.
And, why not -
Are there not tales told by even the most heroic
hunters of dangerous attacks and marauding?
Contending otherwise, she lay there -
imagining the imminence of fur growing
beside her, within herself -

and reaches to his haunch to feel hairiness,
the fuzz of humanness transforming
in the semiconscious, nocturnal groping.

She awakens in the morning to a dream of
her own hirsute and winter-fatted figure -
snarling and growling and crawling
across the quilted lair to embrace the beast.
Now, as the brilliance of daylight pours
in like spring edging into the cave,
he implores her to tell him a story:
the one of a woman who slept beside a bear.

Jennifer Mathews

THE LEDGE

I threw the square of mortar and granite
out to where the ledge drops off.
The truncated block blasted the surface.
Skating bugs scattered, droplets leapt

into the air, sprinkled our toes.
And you dove for it.
Four mouthfuls of air brought you down
and back through refracted sky.

Eyes squinted, palm stretched open
you searched the lake's floor
stirring silt and weightless weeds.
I stood on the float

dry towel on my neck
your t-shirt balled at my feet.
I had promised to be your date
if you could bring it up.

And you had never dived deeper.
I knew the ledge.
I knew the depth
and where, as you groped
the murky sands,

the granite was sinking
through bottle green rays
past vertical intrusions
onto dark currents
far beyond your reach.

A WOMAN'S WORK

It is fine silk she creates within
and spews forth again and again
to make senseless beauty in the world,
hold her children,
and have a quiet something to hold onto.
Her thread is fine, delicate, almost invisible:
>only those that look carefully on dewy mornings
>will see the glory of her creation.

She is always busy:
renewing her inner silk;
repairing this web and that, carelessly torn
>by the wind
>>the unexpected
>>>and those unconscious souls;
She rests, waits
for all that is to come.

She does not tire
knowing the importance of the work:
spinning, mending, tending, waiting,
creating a constant quiet cradle for
the young,
>the fragile being,
>>the dew.

Peter F. McGuire

HOUSE CALL

The house trailer sits on top of the hill.
Tattered curtains wave a welcome from screenless windows.
BEWARE THE DOG is tacked to the scarred maple.
The growling bitch, leashed I hope, lies in the shade
Escaping the humorless August sun.

Blueberry smudge-faced children run and hide
In the old Ford sinking into the goldenrod.
Its rear end is balanced precariously on a rusted jack.
They shoot at me with Mattel M-16's,
Firing my memory of the bunkers of Southeast Asia.

The man, food stained undershirt stretched tight
Over his ascitic abdomen, nods an eyeless greeting
As he shuffles to the garden overrun with pig weed
He kicks the rusted hoe aside. It strikes back
Whacking him in the shin. He curses.

The woman lies on a living room pallet.
Coke cans dribble on the scrap of green carpet.
Shallow breath comes from her bronchitic lungs.
A Marlboro hangs from her yellowed fingers.
It's good of you to come, she whispers.

Susan Nichols

FOR LUCY

Bone fragments
of jaw
thigh
and finger
do not reveal
the heart of my ancient ancestor
in Olduvai Gorge.
Where were you going?
Had you lost a child in birth,
loved a dancing man,
sung to the morning light?
Were you tired of your journey,
afraid you'd lost your way,
grateful for the death that came
in the plain
between here and there?
Covered by earth for the millenia
you appear again, too soon,
my mother,
to raise simple questions.

Walden S.Norton

SCHERAZADE

The small stick-skinny girl twirls in late afternoon light
reflected from shining floors by long windows.
Her toes grab the floor to keep from falling
as the cascades of music push her
to a flinging outstretch of thin arms
to match the music as it flows
beyond the horizon in sheets of colored sound.

Violins rule the newly Russian world.
It is the grandparents' home, and for this moment
she is the center, where the two old ones give what they love
in waves of Rimsky-Korsakov,
resonating off the walls of saved china, books,
Grecian red cut-glass goblets,
the light is dim and enchanting.

The small figure is in a shift of a nightgown.
The old ones have just finished a game of chess.
They sink back in their chairs, and smile.
Dance, they say, dance.
Show what the violins ask-
use your body as a tongue,
says the violinist grandmother.

Each sound goes to the bone.
Oboes call forth yearning that doubles the child
to the floor, in repetitive circles
that widen and decrease to the vibrato.
The child becomes a single clear string,
twisting, fighting, in the grasp of unknown wanting
from some deep place inside.

In silent attention, the old ones watch,
nodding with the pulse of the music,
leaning into the highnotes.
The small muscles strive to tell the tale
of marshaling forces for an unseen battle,
where good stands against evil somehow,
though no one speaks. The violins transcend
drums and clarinets - bugles sound. Responding,
she thrusts upward, frenzied, passionate,
beyond voice and thought. Her skin glistens with sweat,
her frame energized by an empathy so complete
tears fly from her face as fast as they form.

A single concentration grips the room.
The old ones see moving before them
in wispy delicate sweeps the energy of life.
The eight year old dips, gathers herself,
graciously opens her arms to it all,
holds life confidently close, then
in a storm of spins, leaps
to be the tongue of them all.

The orchestra crescendos, the room is too small-
her jumps lose synchronicity as the child dares too much.
Finally, the composer releases them to a more human scale.
The child turns, glowing everywhere,
to take a trembling wet hand and place it
softly on her grandfather's whisker-rough face
for a long stroke as delicate as a breath, and
collapses in tears of exhaustion and delight at his feet.

The two gather the beloved child onto their four knees,
and together the three cling, transported,
in the late afternoon twilight,
after chess,
as the sun goes down.

Patty Olds

THE PART OF THE DAUGHTER

He lost his job his car broke down the pipes burst his dog died
the bank foreclosed he's talking suicide
and she calls me to come make it better
Because I've only got one father, as if anyone would want two
as if the threat of extinction has anything to do with love
As if love is grounds for blackmail
As if I could choose against the bribe.

Of course I care. Of course I'll come. He is my father. I owe him.
I say these things to her in more languages than I know.
Crescendo, diminuendo.
Blood is thicker than chickens. Don't count your water.
A stitch in time saves. When is it time for a new coat?
I do not have answers for him, will not pretend otherwise,
but I'll show him my maps, play him my music, feed him my food.
Let him see how creative his genes can be, given the chance.

David Polsky

GRANDFATHER POEM

Years after your hands stopped lifting pencils,
stopped tying shoes, they remained muscular,
wide and intimidating little pit bulls
I could hold in my hands and feel
the hard rubber of superballs inside,
as though someone had stuffed them
till they bulged, till your fingers
stuck out stiff with the memory
of holding knives, lifting dead animals,
dismantling their bodies, cleaving the flesh
of cows from the bone as though
undressing a stubborn child.

Sometimes I would place my hand in yours
as though flirting with danger, as if
a freak synapse might misfire, closing your hand
shut in a flash, crushing my fingers
like a handful of twigs. Sometimes I watched
your hands while you ate. They would
flop and twitch in your lap like fish.

Your head, dropped back in your wheelchair,

held eyes which said you were somewhere else,

somewhere inside keeping the company

of your disease; watching the Parkinson's

cleave you from your body

one nerve at a time, as you

on your hands and knees

groped for your knife in the dark.

FIREWALK

I hear the fears of others:
fear of the fire itself,
fear of falling, burning.
But mostly they are fears within.
Some need to get rid of anger.
Pain. Grief. Guilt.
One says if she can walk on fire,
she can do anything.

I remember the fire of the words
my son spoke four years ago
when I left his father and my family.
He said I ran away, that I didn't face up
to the problems, that I took the easy way out.
The heat of anger in his voice ignited me
with the fear that I might lose him.
More fear and pain
than even fire could bring.

I step up to the coals. I look up.
I breathe deeply and feel love.
I think hummingbirds, my grandson's favorite bird.
I become part of the fire.
This is easy compared to the fear I knew.

Walter Rattan

SECOND HUSBAND

He went away slowly,
as the dead always do
who've been well loved.

First, of course, the suit
she buried him in,
gray on a gray day.

Then the clothes the boys took.
Why not use what you can?
No good hanging here,

leaking memories
and losing his shape.
The rest for Goodwill.

Tangible reminders gone,
phantoms kept returning, like
the pain from a lost limb;

the laugh wrinkles in his eyes,
his hungry touch in the night,
his footstep on the stair.

At last she couldn't hear that anymore,
and the lawyers, solemn and solicitous,
intoned their last pronouncements.

Her closet empty, Ned came;
slowly, as the other had left,
and as quietly, occupying certain

vacancies, including her body;
accepting that others
must remain unfilled.

Three years now, and little remains
of the other except the boys,
the oak tree in the yard,

and a photograph, buried in a trunk
under her off-season clothes,
exhumed occasionally in quiet contemplation.

Alice V. Rohman

IN THE AFTERNOON LIGHT

That empty chair holds stillness -
      and the hollow of a back.
Palm oils have greased the arms,
      and spare wooden legs
      are fixed fast to the floor.

It seems to be waiting.
I sense it has always been here,
      or always there,
      and not waiting.
Just ready,
      just open,
          just available.

Just now, the light slanted perfectly,
      and I was chair-like.
I swear two spirits spoke.

Jean Scudder

CROW'S NEST

Your words are like the woodsman's wedge;
well placed, firmly struck;

Perched, precipitous, I sway
from them, until little bits of camouflage,
glittering tin baubles
begin to drop;
Then larger,
whizzing, spinning and changing to dust;
All angles, mirrors, deflectors,
bits of familiar frippery,
fat wads of stuffing, slough off with soft whumps
of dacron lining, cotton fuzzing, thick
glutinous dough layers deep;

I fly in frantically with new bits,
shreds of scratched reruns,
shoulder pads, foil, radar deflectors,
comments on the news, the weather;
Anything to keep you from getting me;
Afraid even my blackness will be gone
when you stop,
stumped, empty handed
staring
at feathers and air.

THE DEATH OF JOHN A. SPENKELINK

Appeals were depleted—
Spenkelink rode the lightning,
strapped into Old Sparky
on a platform in a little beige room,
his chin locked in a steel trap,
he sat like a king,
an emperor of ice cream.

A new suit of clothes, black mask,
shaved and greased above the ankle,
wet sponge of saline attached
to the metal cap atop his head;
he could drink all the sodas he wanted,
water is a good conductor, they said.

The executioner was a few feet away
in his switchbooth,
power surged in his killing hand
as a preacher read from the Holy Bible.
Imploring the witnesses with his eyes
fear streamed in the face of the condemned man.

His scream was heard through the Everglades

as the ends of his fingers curled

and smoke poured from the wire at his right ankle.

Stench of burned flesh filled the chamber

as the doctor applied his cold stethoscope

declaring the prisoner dead

at 10:18 A.M.

The reporters paled and left the witness room,

called their respective papers

and wrote up the story of how

death comes in oak wood.

Connie M. Sexton

CAPTIVATED

Nostalgia, prison of the sentimental,
hinders progressive reasoning,
backtracks winding useless memories
through inconsequential reverie.

Nostalgia justifies an allegiance
to brown liquid
refrigerated in a gleaming metal cup
for fourteen years,
the coffee her son poured
the day of his death.

An octogenarian friend requested
that her icebox be tidied.
I found the coffee,
tightly covered,
in the door shelf.

The ruby aluminum tumbler,
scratched but still shiny,
retrieved my recollections
of the tumbler status symbol.

Bright hued tumblers, emblems
of modern housekeeping,
did not break and
kept iced tea cold
on a hot summer's day.

Ours were hammered aluminum,
revealing the imprints of formation
into cylinders most useful,
distinctly special,
but not color-tinged,
barely acceptable substitutes.

I asked my friend,
the owner of the coffee,
about its destiny.
"Throw it out,"
was her pained reply.

A wise decision,
declared the logic of my brain,
but passion and sentiment
challenged the notion.

I poured it down the sink,
the last of Harold's blood,
gone into the sewer.

I searched the face of my friend
for fresh wounds or old scar tissue.
She revealed relief.

Held prisoner by the coffee,
she could never liberate herself.

I left for the day,
accompanied by a discarded,
antiquated bottle
of Worcestershire.
"I collect old bottles,"
I said aimlessly,
knowing the cell walls
had surrounded me.

GAY IRIS

A sixty year old gay man,
my former landlord,
gave me iris from beds
he tended on a ridge
overlooking the South Branch
of the Potomac. He dug tubers
up, broke them off, inquiring,
"What colors, my boy, do you
want? The yellows? They
are luscious. Or blues?
I love them. Or reds?
Just look at them!" I took
three paper bags, each full
of iris, put them in my car
and returned for a swim.

Aged, wrinkled but hot as ever
for my body, he watched me swim
in the river, float as I used to float
when I was twenty-three
when he lured young men
my age and younger to the house,

and introduced me, invited me
to the main part—his part—
of the house. "To eat with them."
He wanted me to fall in love
with one of them, to convert
to homosexuality like one
who'd found religion.

The iris I took to Maine,
planted in the back yard
in a semi-circle. After
one dormant year they are pursed,
their tight green lips
like tips of erect penises
bent to the new sun.

He'd be proud the way I care
for them, feed them 5-10-5,
clip them back after tumescence.
It's the way he wanted me to hold
his member when, in bright afternoons,
lonely, waist deep in the river
I heard from the house his cum cries
and dove under the rapid water,
swam against the current
to test if I could outlast it.

Jeri Theriault

WHAT I NEED

First...a doctor to tell
me what the heart truly is.
(A rock, I think, marbled with mica
and cold lines, dense as a diamond.)
A doctor would tell me that the duodenum
is the sack of throbs, full of something
churning like love.

I need an accountant.
A man to give me the numbers
I forget, someone to count syllables.
And I need a chemist to tell me what exactly
happens at the boiling point.

(You will notice I said "a man."
I'm being practical, not sexist.
If any of these were women, we'd
end up talking about feelings and cycles
over endless cups of tea. A man can stay
in one room marked "logic" for twelve hours,
make love, take a shower, and return to his tickertape
of definitions, humming.
That's the kind of dedication I need.)

I need a carpenter to build

a bench in the garden. To tell me how many

support beams Aphrodite's library had.

And a mechanic to discuss this trembling idle,

new brakes, exhaust systems. (Think

of the metaphors I could make from the plastic

gloves and ledgers, the beakers

boiling, the wires and screws.)

Maybe what I really need

are just the parts, all of them together

in a cage, pulsing

like digestive organs, soft,

malleable, nothing like a heart,

(nothing.)

SEA MONKEYS

She did wear awful shoes,
red rubber shoes from the Jewel man
who sold door to door,
shoes that seemed to stretch
so that, even at twelve,
she couldn't escape the wretched things.
At church, the nice girls laughed,
and I shut up and never said
how much I loved her,
or how she pulled "Shenandoah"
from the worn strings of her violin.
At her house children ate
whole jars of jam with their fingers.
One sister started fucking at ten.
The youngest tore the arms and legs
off all the dolls.
And while the church girls
were leaping from cheer to cheer
with their beautiful legs,
and learning to curl hair
into perfect pageboys and flips,

she and I tried to grow Sea Monkeys,

praying that the hidden creatures

would grow into trainable beings

that whirled and tumbled

to our simple commands.

Judy Torrico

CERTAINLY THIS ISN'T

the first time it has rained
since you have been gone.
Why do I ache in those places
you used
to brush softly and call your own.

Still the moon sits
silver on the elm.
It pulses behind drifting clouds and
displays a damaged face.

A toad jumps, belly pressed to the glass
exposing the pale pulse
that clings to the warmth.

Something sticks, ugly as loneliness,
in my throat, I feel it
throb and hesitate,
desiring your return.

Not for the first time
since you left, I watch
the night croak at morning.

SOME BIRDS

As much as I want the dream,
it escapes. There is no cardinal
at the feeder when I wake, my
body a language
whose tongue has flown away.

Like rain.
This mockingbird
pelts my window, makes
territory. As if each shriek
could silence his bickering reflection.
How does he know he's won
when he furls his white bars
and makes his tail small, begins
his Berlitz
from thick green spoils?

I am listening to Mozart
when the finches return — such
happy birds — downstairs repotting
the furry streptocarpus.
This crown tears apart
like green wings,
or tongues.

See how my clumps of earth
and sharp knife,
my blackened hands and hammer —
see how my red shards fly.

Gaylord Day Weston

BURYING MOTHER

I'm carrying Mother around
in my trunk, these days,
everywhere I go, so I don't forget
to take her to Connecticut for a proper burial.

There's so much to remember—
make hotel reservations,
pack funeral clothes,
and bathing suits (there's a pool),
bring cigarettes—
they're wicked expensive in Connecticut—
dog to the kennel,
coordinate the cat sitters,
hold the mail,
check the oil, leave by 7:00 a.m., two cars, smokers,
non-smokers, six people.

Sometimes I forget
she's there.
In the trunk.

For a while I couldn't remember

the date we set for

the trek to the Merwin plot

to bury Mother.

Those few weeks of her dying

-between Thanksgiving and Christmas, last year—

encompassed our only time of loving

I can remember.

It was a pure, sweet time

but too short

to lose resentments, angers.

Maybe she should have died sooner

and taken longer.

I don't know.

I only know Mother's in the trunk

and I hate to look inside.

THE LANGUAGE OF THE MIDDLE BODY

I wish that we
could be
decapitated,
guillotined in mid-sentence;
your yammering head
would roll to the left,
mine to the right.
We'd sit
cross-legged and
contemplate
our headlessness,
try to rest our
non-existent chins
on our fists.
We'd speak
the language
of the middle body,
each organ
vibrating the air
with private messages:
boisterous whoops from the genitals,
breathy whispers from expanding lungs,

explosive barks from your rectum,

playful growls from my stomach

and over all,

the gently drumming dialogue

of our sympathetic hearts.

Douglas Woodsum

PITCHER PLANTS IN JANUARY

Betrayed by a thirst, the pitcher
Plants stand as if alive, frozen erect.
Subtle meat-eaters, they wait,

Killers and trappers, hunters that are urns,
Thin-skinned with red veins even in winter,
Dead now. Diluted enzymes and nectar

Freezes, a crystal web of water.
A pool of rain holds
The petal-rimmed shapes hard as shell,

Ice keeping things whole.
It is too cold for insects now. Only
A chickadee pecks the ice inside

A flowering stomach. Between the woods
And frozen pond, preserved pitcher plants
Rise —above brittle grasses and leaves—

Swaying in breezes on thin stems.
They must thaw and live again. Death has been
Too kind to them; there must be another.

EPILOGUE

EPILOGUE

Most of us know the urge to write and long for the excitement of connecting the right words on the page before us. To capture a remembrance, to record a discovery or moment of despair. We each seek that sense of discovering, as Frost said, something we didn't know we knew. It may end there, in a journal, a letter to a friend. For most of us write these thoughts for ourselves, or those we love.

But this book brings together the work of poets who are reaching out to a larger audience, beyond the safe center of friend and home. And these poets have, in their journeys, turned to writing workshops offered by Maine Writers & Publishers Alliance. I hope they found support in these workshops, though perhaps not always in the way they expected. I hope they were challenged to beyond their expectations of themselves and I hope they benefited from the insights of their peers and their gifted and dedicated teachers.

As I write this, the alliance is entering its twentieth year. In December, 1974, a group of writers and small press publishers got together for the first time to share ideas and to look for ways of reaching a larger audience for their work. Through these years MWPA has grown and its programs now include writing workshops, an annual Fall Writing Retreat, a monthly newsletter: *Maine In Print,* an annual chapbook competition, a book distribution service, and more.

Though twenty years have passed, these goals remain central to MWPA: to support the creative work of Maine's writers and publishers, to connect them with one another and with the public. This book is, I hope, a small symbol of that work, a reflection of writers coming together to support one another, to learn from one another, to develop their craft, and ultimately, to reach you. But you, I hope, will not see this book so much as a symbol as an invitation. Keep reading, keep writing.

Harriet Mosher
Executive Director, MWPA

Jean Fahringer graduated from Swarthmore College in 1930. She was a reader, writer, and lover of poetry her whole life. Apparently while at Swarthmore, she worked with an artist friend to produce a hand-written, hand-sewn book of her favorite poems by Edna St. Vincent Millay. The book is illustrated with original paintings by an artist who is identified only by the initials R.S. on each picture. My mother's college friends and sister have no memory of this book, of a friend with the initials R.S., or, in fact, of any acquaintance who was a painter. With regret I can only credit the illustrator of <u>Untidy Candles</u> with these initials and hope that R.S. would be pleased to see his or her work grace these pages and reach a new generation of poetry lovers.

J.Z.